WHAT COMPAI... LITERATURE?

CW00918996

An Inaugural Lecture delivered before the University of Oxford on 11 October 1994 by

GEORGE STEINER

Lord Weidenfeld Visiting Professor of European Comparative Literature

CLARENDON PRESS · OXFORD

1995

Oxford University Press, Walton Street, Oxford OX2 6DP

Oxford New York
Athens Auckland Bangkok Bombay
Calcutta Cape Town Dar es Salaam Delhi
Florence Hong Kong Istanbul Karachi
Kuala Lumpur Madras Madrid Melbourne
Mexico City Nairobi Paris Singapore
Taipei Tokyo Toronto

and associated companies in
Berlin Ibadan

Oxford is a trade mark of Oxford University Press

Published in the United States
by Oxford University Press Inc., New York

British Library Cataloguing in Publication Data
Data available

Library of Congress Cataloging in Publication Data
Data available
ISBN 0-19-952268-5

1 3 5 7 9 10 8 6 4 2

Set by Hope Services (Abingdon) Ltd.
Printed in Great Britain by
Oxuniprint
Oxford University Press
Walton Street
Oxford

WHAT IS COMPARATIVE LITERATURE?

EVERY act of the reception of significant form, in language, in art, in music, is comparative. Cognition is re-cognition, either in the high Platonic sense of a remembrance of prior truths, or in that of psychology. We seek to understand, to 'place' the object before us—the text, the painting, the sonata—by giving it the intelligible, informing context of previous and related experience. We look, intuitively, to analogy and precedent, to the traits as of a family (thus 'familiar') which relate the work that is new to us to a recognizable context. In the case of radical innovation, of a poetic or representational or musical structure which strikes us as in some ways unprecedented, the process of response is a complex motion towards the incorporation of the new into the known. Even extreme originality begins, as we enter into questioning dialogue with it, to tell of origins. There is in the perception of and response to intelligibility no absolute innocence, no Adamic nakedness. Interpretation and aesthetic judgement, however spontaneous in utterance, however provisional or even misguided, arise from an echo-chamber of historical, social, technical presuppositions and recognizance. (Here, the legal sense of this term is pertinent: a certain contract of eventual decipherment, of informed evaluation underwrites the encounter between our sensibility and the text or work of art.) In this dynamic process, called 'hermeneutic' perhaps after Hermes, god of messages and fictions, comparison is implicit. How does this novel or symphony relate to what we have previously read or heard, to our expectations in respect of executive form? The notion of 'making new' (Ezra Pound's injunction) is comparative in logic and substance. Newer than what? There are, even at the sharpest pitch of the revolutionary, no utter 'singularities'. We soon learn to hear the part of Brahms in Schoenberg, to observe the lit shadows of Manet in Rothko. The barest assertion of preference is precisely that: a comparison with. It may well be that the reflexes that put in play similarity and dissimilarity, analogy, and contrast are fundamental to the human psyche and to the possibility of the intelligible. French makes this audible: in 'reason', *raison*, 'comparison', *comparaison*, is instrumental.

Given language, it cannot be otherwise. Each word in either an oral or written communication reaches us charged with the potential of its entire history. All previous uses of this word or phrase are implicit or, as the physicists would say, 'implosive' in it. We know strictly nothing of its invention except where it is a neologism or technical term whose first appearance we can more or less confidently document. Who devised, who used for the very first time the words which articulate our consciousness and organize our relations to the world and to each other? Who originated the similes, the metaphors which encode the unfolding of our perceptions, which make the sea 'wine-dark' or set the number of the stars in concordance with that of the grains of sand? Our recursion, up-stream, to the sources of saying is, almost always, partial. We are unable to date, to situate geographically, let alone in some individual act of perception and enunciation, the first light in language. For even the most anarchic, innovative of writers, the linguistic and, to a large extent, the grammatical building blocks are already there, crowded with historical, literary, and idiomatic resonance.

The classic artist rejoices in this inheritance. He moves into a house richly furnished, its mirrors, as it were, radiant with the presence of preceding tenants. The counter-classic writer finds himself in a veritable prison-house of language. *In extremis*, we know of drastic attempts at escape. The Dada movement, Surrealism, Russian Futurist verse experiment, quite desperately, with the concoction of new languages, of non-sense discourse or, in the Russian case, 'star-speech'. Not only are these contrivances haunted by the spectral force of the syllables, of the words they seek to discard; but they are unintelligible. If a poet was able to construe a new language and syntax he would, in order to be understood, have to teach it first to himself, then to another. In which 'loquacious' motion the prison-house would begin to be built. When Joyce, in his copy of *Finnegans Wake*, lists some forty tongues from which he has made the collages of his word-play, macaronics or acrostics, he does so in the knowledge that the history of these languages and their literary and public use press on even the most *outré* of his inventions. At best, the major writer adds graffiti to the walls of the already extant house of language. In turn, these graffiti enlarge the walls and further complicate their echoes.

Linguistically, we come to grasp and use words diacritically, which is to say by virtue of what differentiates them from other words. In poetics, as Coleridge argues in the *Biographia Litteraria*, both understanding and pleasure derive from the tensed imbalance between the expected and the shock of the new, which is itself, at its finest, a shock of recognition, a *déjà vu*. The poet's language takes us home to that which we did not know. It is in this precise psychological and epistemological sense that the 'Library at Babel' (Borges) and, above all, its dictionaries, do contain the totality of literatures past, present, and to come. The semantic process is one of differentiation. To read is to compare.

From their inception, literary studies and the arts of interpretation have been comparative. The pedagogues, the textual commentators, the literary critics, and theoreticians of Athens and Alexandria compare diverse aspects within the works of a single writer, such as Homer. They observe the dynamics of analogy and contrast between the treatment of identical mythological themes by different tragedians such as Aeschylus, Sophocles, and Euripides. As Latin literature develops, linguistic-critical comparisons between Homer and Virgil, between Roman pastorale and its Greek-Hellenic inspiration, between Herodotus and Roman historians, become the commonplace of the curriculum and of the teaching of rhetoric. Plutarch's 'pairings' of a Greek and a Roman statesman, legislator or man of war are exemplary of a comparative method also used in the study of writers and rhetoricians. Soon centuries of clerics and of schoolboys were to toil over the comparison of Cicero with Demosthenes, of Virgil with Theocritus, of Seneca with Euripides. And it does not escape the polemic notice of early adversaries of Christianity that the scenario of agonized death and glorious resurrection is comparatively discernible in the myths of Osiris or Adonis.

Aesthetic judgement, hermeneutic exposition by way of comparison—Dryden and Pope, as seen by Dr Johnson; Corneille and Racine as read by Boileau; Shakespeare and Racine in Stendhal's polemic—is a constant in literary study and debate. Techniques of intra- and inter-linguistic confrontation are sharpened during the quarrels between 'Ancients' and 'Moderns' in the seventeenth and eighteenth centuries and by the reprise of this quarrel in the late eighteenth- and nineteenth-century conflicts between romanticism and various modes of neo-classicism. Wordsworth is a comparatist in action when he seeks to dismantle a text by Gray in the Preface to the *Lyrical Ballads*; Victor Hugo is a comparatist when he invokes Aeschylus, the *Book of Job*, and Shakespeare against Racine in the programmatic Preface to *Cromwell*.

Weltliteratur ('world-literature') is Goethe's coinage. We find it for the first time in a diary entry for 15 January 1827. But it formulates intimations and practices which span Goethe's lifetime. Goethe translates out of eighteen languages including Gaelic, Arabic, Chinese, Hebrew, Persian, and Finnish (to be sure, the translation is often indirect and at second-hand). These translations span seventy-three years, from a fragment from Lipsius' Latin in 1757 to extracts from Carlyle's life of Schiller which he translates in 1830. European awareness owes to Goethe some of its seminal moments of translation: that of Cellini's autobiography, of Voltaire's *Mahomet*, of Diderot's *Neveu de Rameau*. Within Goethe's own poetry, the *West-Östlicher Divan*, adapted from the Persian, the version of the *Song of Songs* from the Hebrew, or the translation and 're-composition' from the Italian of Manzoni's ode *Il Cinque Maggio*, represent sovereign achievements. The theoretical programme for the translator set out in the Introduction to the *Divan* is one of the most demanding and influential in the long history of the craft.

But the study and practice of translation is only a part of the concept of *Weltliteratur*. Behind the word lies *Weltpoesie*, an expression rooted in the conceptions of language and of literature put forward by Herder and Humboldt. The faculty for, the impulse towards verbal invention, towards the organization of words and syntax into formal patterns of measure and musicality, is universal. *Poiesis*, the ordering *ingenium* which gives to the world a narrative guise, which concentrates and dramatizes the raw material of experience, which translates grief and wonder into aesthetic pleasure, is ubiquitous. Man is not only, as the ancient Greeks had it, 'a language-animal'; he is a being in whom greater or lesser degrees of formal imagining and stylized communication are innate. In Goethe's view, all modes of literary enunciation, oral or written, are of cardinal relevance to man's understanding of his history, of his civil condition and, strikingly, of his own language. 'He who does not know foreign languages,' rules Goethe, 'knows nothing of his own.'

The entailments of *Weltliteratur* are also philosophical and political. Goethe was, we know, obsessed by the quest for primordial unities. Tenaciously, he pursued the chimera of the *Ur-pflanze*, the vegetable form from which all other species would evolve. *Faust II* is, in several respects, the inspiration for subsequent notions of 'archetypes', of original and originating configurations in the final deeps of nascent consciousness (Jung is steeped in Goethe). Like the alchemists, whom he read closely, Goethe believed in the interrelationships, in the hidden harmonies of all matter. The voice of nature was best audible in great chords and unison. *Weltliteratur* and *Weltpoesie* connote a conjecture, though indistinct, as to the universals which underlie and generate all languages and which occasion, between even the most formally remote, subterranean structural and evolutionary affinities. Goethe's ecumenism implies a moral-political stance. By the late 1820s, the ageing and partially isolated Olympian—isolated by his world-fame—had a vivid apprehension of the new forces of nationalism, of militant chauvinism on the march in post-Napoleonic Europe, and especially in Germany. He knew and feared the Teutonic verbiage and archaicizing fervour of the new German philology and historiography. Thus the late coinage, *Weltliteratur*, seeks to articulate ideals, attitudes of sensibility which belong to the universalizing civilities, to the international freemasonry of enlightened spirits characteristic of the Enlightenment. The study of other languages and literary traditions, the appreciation both of their intrinsic value and of that which interweaves them with the sum of the human condition, 'enriches' that condition. It is integral to 'free trade' in an intellectual and spiritual sense. In the life of the mind, as in that of politics, isolationism and nationalist arrogance are the road to brutal ruin.

It is these persuasions and the poetic-critical realization which Goethe gave them, that lay the express foundation for comparative literature. They are its ideals of responsibility still.

The history of comparative literature as a professional and academic discipline is a complex and, in some measure, a sombre one. It is made up of accidents of personal and social circumstance together with larger currents of a cognitive and historical nature. The interactions between these generative elements are so manifold and, at points, opaque as to rebuke any attempt at a brief or confident summation. A field or manner of study, of reading, of secondary discourse (edition, commentary, critical classification) becomes a visible entity in the modern scholastic-academic edifice when it produces books explicit to itself, when it establishes university chairs, journals, and a syllabus. In steps at first tentative and almost unnoticed, comparative literature begins to accede to these criteria around the turn of the century. Its immediate backdrop is that of Franco-German tensions, particularly in Alsatia and the Rhineland, between the end of the Franco-Prussian war and the outbreak of the First World War (which was, as we ought never to forget, a European civil war). Almost every psychological, geographical, and topical aspect I have touched upon is crystallized in the fact that one of the very first books of modern comparative literature in any self-conscious vein should have been Fernand Baldensperger's *Goethe en France* of 1904. Nor is it an accident that it was from a German reading of French literature and from an endeavour to re-define the *Latinitas* primary to Europe before divisive nationalism that came such classic work in comparative literature as that of E. R. Curtius and Leo Spitzer. No less crucial is a related but tragic component.

It is no secret that Jewish scholars or scholars of Jewish origin have played an often preponderant role in the development of comparative literature as an academic-critical pursuit. One is indeed tempted to associate the early history of the subject with the crisis of fact and of mood triggered by the Dreyfus Affair. Endowed, it would appear, with an unusual facility for languages, compelled to be a *frontalier* (the grim Swiss word for those who, materially and psychologically dwell near or astride borders), the twentieth-century Jew would be drawn naturally to a comparative view of the secular literatures which he treasured but in none of which he was natively or 'by right of national inheritance' altogether at home. Driven into exile—the masterpiece of modern comparative literature, Auerbach's *Mimesis* was written in Turkey by a refugee deprived, overnight of his livelihood, first language, and library—the Jews (my own teachers) fortunate enough to reach North America, would find traditional departments of literature, departments of English first and foremost, barred to them. Thus much of what became comparative literature programmes or departments in American academe arose from marginalization, from partial social and ethnic exclusion. (There are fascinating parallels in the case of atomic physics in the United States.) Comparative literature therefore carries within it both the virtuosities and the sadness of a certain exile, of an inward *diaspora*. I need hardly say that it is this central truth which renders so particularly apt and comely Lord Weidenfeld's generosity in establishing this visiting chair and the honour accorded to me in inviting me to be its first incumbent.

In a characteristically American scenario, the pursuit of comparative literature rapidly became professionalized and organizational. Professorships, journals, specialized library-resources, doctoral dissertations flourished. This floruit may already be over. With the natural deaths of the refugee-masters, the polyglot requisites, the Greek-Latin and Hebraic background, the obvious necessity, wherever practicable, of reading texts in the original, have ebbed. In too many universities and colleges, comparative literature today is conducted, if at all, nearly entirely via translation. The amalgamation with threatened departments of modern languages, with 'core-courses' on Western civilization and with the new demands for pan-ethnicity, for 'global' studies, lies readily to hand. In more and more curricula, 'comparative literature' has come to signify 'a reading of great books which one ought to have read anyway in, preferably paperback and in the Anglo-American tongue'. Or a resolve, assuredly arguable, to set classics too long prepotent, too long dusty beside, often in the boisterous shadow of, the Afro-American, the Chicano, the Amazonian traditions (a displacement which already tempted that brilliant comparatist, Maurice Bowra).

More traditional teaching of and research into comparative literature flourishes, at present, in the sometime communist sphere. Certain centres in Russia and Eastern Europe are among the most productive and convinced. Here again, a natural necessity for the acquisition of languages, a bitter experience of exile, be it internal, an often vexed questioning of historical, linguistic identity, makes of the comparative approach a relevant method. But prophecies are idle. What can be ventured is this: the instauration of this visiting professorship at Oxford, the hope that a full and professorial programme in comparative literature—and not only European—will follow, do coincide with a time of some uncertainty, potentially fruitful, in this subject.

But *is* it a subject? Can it distinguish itself from the practices of comparison, of parallel and contrastive readings and reception which I have briefly mentioned and with are a natural

part of all informed literacy? Is the comparatist, in any professional, entitled sense, a man or woman who will (who should)
wake up one morning knowing that he or she, just like
Molière's Monsieur Jourdain, has, like all his colleagues, been
'speaking prose'?

The brief replies I want to try and give to this insistent
question are bound to be tentative. They are inevitably personal. They cannot hope to speak for this hybrid and protean
field as a whole. May Goethe be my guide when he avows, in
a Yiddish of Frankfurt provenance, that 'every man prophesies
out of his own little book'!

In the humanities (proud, sad word), aspirations to system-
atic definition end, virtually always, in sterile tautology.
'Theory' has its precise meaning and criteria of falsifiability in
the sciences. This is not so in the humanities where claims to
the 'theoretical' produce, as we know to our current cost, arro-
gant jargon. In reference to literary and aesthetic experience
and judgement, 'theory' is nothing but subjective intuition or
descriptive narrative grown impatient. Pascal reminds us: the
sphere of finesse is not that of geometry.

I take comparative literature to be, at best, an exact and
exacting art of reading, a style of listening to oral and written
acts of language which privileges certain components in these
acts. Such components are not neglected in any mode of literary study, but they are, in comparative literature, privileged.

Any reading engages the history and tenets of language.
Comparative literature, while alert to the contributions of formal and abstract linguistics, is immersed in, delights in, the
prodigal diversity of natural languages. Comparative literature
listens and reads after Babel. It posits the intuition, the hypoth-
esis that, far from being a disaster, the multiplicity of human
tongues, some twenty thousand of which have, at various
times, been spoken on this small planet, has been the enabling
condition of men and women's freedom to perceive, to
articulate, to 're-draft' the existential world in manifold freedom. Each and every language construes the facticity of existential reality, of 'the given' (*les données immédiates*) in its own

specific way. Each and every window in the house of languages opens on to a different landscape and temporality, to a
different segmentation in the spectrum of perceived and
classified experience. No language divides time or space
exactly as does any other (consider Hebrew verb-tenses, if one
can speak of such); no language has identical taboos with any
other (hence the profound Don Juanism of making love in different tongues); no language dreams precisely like any other.
The extinction of a language, however remote, however
immune to historical-material success or diffusion, is the
death of a unique world-view, of a genre of remembrance,
of present being and of futurity. A truly dead language is
irreplaceable. It closes that which Kierkegaard bade us keep
open if our humanity was to evolve: 'the wounds of possibility'.
Such closure may, for late twentieth-century mass-media
and mass-market technocracy, be a triumph. It may facilitate
the *imperium* of the fast-food chain and the news-satellite.
For the lessening chances of the human spirit, it is destruc-
tive.

Jubilant at the intractable diversity of Babel, comparative literature privileges a twofold principle. It aims to elucidate the
quiddity, the autonomous core of historical and present 'sense
of the world' (Husserl's *Weltsinn*) in the language and to clarify,
so far as is possible, the conditions, the strategies, the limits of
reciprocal understanding and misunderstanding as between languages. In brief, comparative literature is an art of understanding centred in the eventuality and defeats of translation. I have
tried to show elsewhere that this process begins within the same
language, that individuals, generations, genders, social classes,
professions, ideologies, past and present, 'translate' when they
would understand any communicative discourse inside their
own tongue. This immensely complex, ontologically enigmatic
process—how is it that they do understand and decipher one
another, even if always imperfectly?—becomes fully visible and
crucial inter-lingually, across language boundaries.

Every facet of translation—its history, its lexical and grammatical means, the differences of approach that extend from

the word-by-word interlinear to the freest imitation or meta-
morphic adaptation—is absolutely pivotal to the comparatist.
The commerce between tongues, between texts of different historical periods or literary forms, the complex interactions
between a new translation and those that have gone before,
the ancient but always vivid contest of ideals as between the
'letter' and the 'spirit', is that of comparative literature itself.
To study, say, some of the more than one hundred versions
into English of the *Iliad* and the *Odyssey*, is to experience the
development of the English language from Caxton to Walcott
(one should say 'languages'); it is to gain insight into the successive, constantly altering relations between British sensibility
and representations of the ancient world; it is to observe Pope
reading Chapman and Dryden as readers of Homer, and Pope
himself reading Homer as through the glass brightly of Virgil.
To consider Pound's *Cathay* or Christopher Logue's work-in-
progress on an *Iliad*, is to meet head-on the outrageous miracle
of supreme translation made in ignorance of the relevant language, made by some osmosis of insight which might, if only
we knew how it works, take us to the very heart of the mystery
of language itself. It is, furthermore a close hearing of the fail-
ures or incompletions of even the finest of translations which,
more than any other means of access, helps us throw light on
the life-giving residue of the untranslatable, on the *genius loci* as
it were, in any language. Labour as we may, *bread* will never
wholly translate *pain*. What, in English, French, or Italian is
Heimat?

This primacy of the matter of translation in comparative literature relates directly to what I take to be a second focus. It
is that of the dissemination and reception of literary works
across time and place. The hoary topic of 'influence' is neces-
sarily vague. Writers have heard of, have 'taken from the air'
and surrounding climate of notice, books they have not read.
But the careful investigation of the history of publication
(which may go back to the rolls inscribed or dictated by
Heraclitus), of the sale and transport of books and periodicals,
of library facilities or the absence thereof in any given period

and locale, are vitally illuminating. Who read, who could read what and when? What excerpts, reviews, citations, and translations of the German idealists were actually available to Coleridge? How much did Dostoevsky actually know of Dickens or Balzac? How long—the question busied Nabokov in his magisterial, querulous edition of *Eugene Onegin*—did it take for French translation-imitations of Byron to reach the Caucasus? Had Shakespeare any acquaintance with the opening books of Chapman's 'Homer' when he composed *Troilus and Cressida*?

The obverse seems to me an equally significant question. Why do certain authors, works, literary movements 'pass' (to use a French idiom) whereas others remain stubbornly native? For all his immeasurable verbal, syntactical complication, Shakespeare 'passes', even at the level of the comic-book, into the world's languages. Racine, whom I believe to be wholly comparable in dramatic strength and, at times, more adult by virtue of his matchless economy, does not. Thomas Otway's *Titus and Berenice* of 1676 is just about the only inspired attempt in English to come to 'transferable' terms with the towering fact of Racine. Sir Walter Scott lies at the source of romantic historicism from Madrid to Odessa. The greatest of English novelists, George Eliot, remains an essentially domestic presence. No less instructive are the examples of overestimate, the exaltation of a writer beyond his true and native rank by way of translation or *mimesis*. Poe is a major poet-thinker from Baudelaire and Mallarmé to Valéry. Charles Morgan enters the French Academy. Deconstruction is a fundamentalist faith on the campuses of Nebraska.

There are no ready explanations. Intrinsic linguistic difficulty does not seem in any way causal: look at Urquhart's 'Rabelais' or at German, Italian, and French renderings of Joyce's *Ulysses*; consider Pierre Leiris's resplendent French versions of Gerard Manley Hopkins. Sometimes the accident may be one of biography: had Roy Campbell lived to carry out his recurrent intention of translating Camoëns's *Lusiades*, one of the masterpieces of European literature could well be part of the Anglo-American canon of recognition. Too often, we simply do not know a good reason. But the phenomenology of the untranslatable, the untranslated, the 'unreceived' (*le non-recevoir*) is one of the subtlest of challenges in comparative studies.

A banal but imperative footnote attaches to these two privileged interests. No comparative literature scholar or teacher knows enough languages. Roman Jakobson was reputed to know seventeen, but 'all in Russian'. René Etiemble insisted that even a 'Europeanist' must have knowledge of Chinese and Arabic. For the vast majority among us, such requirements are reproachful dreams or reminders of Joseph Needham! But it is just because much of his work will draw on translations, be it only from the Hebrew Bible, that the comparatist will, at every stage, be intensely responsive to those very matters of translation and dissemination which I have pointed to.

Thematic studies form a third 'centre of gravity' in comparative literature. Analysis, notably by Russian formalists and structural anthropologists, has confirmed the remarkable economy of motifs the recurrent, rule-bound techniques of narrative which prevail in mythologies, folk-tales, and the telling of stories in literature the world over. Tales of triadic temptations and choices, as between three roads, three caskets, three sons, three daughters, three possible brides relate Oedipus to King Lear, Lear to the Karamazov family, and countless variants of this root-structure to the tale of Cinderella. It has been argued that there is, as Robert Graves pronounced, 'one story, and one story only': that of 'The Quest'. The episode of avenging execution in Micky Spillane's *I, The Jury* may derive its undeniable power from that ritual slaying of the priest-king whose global ramifications Frazer sought to inventory in his *Golden Bough*. In the West, twentieth-century art, music, film, literature have returned incessantly to classical mythology: to Oedipus, to Elektra, to Medea, to Odysseus, to Narcissus, to Hercules, or Helen of Troy. My study of *Antigones* appeared in 1984. It is already out of date. A dozen further scenic, narrative, lyric treatments of this 'sad song' (Chaucer's tag) have appeared since. A recent bibliography of the Faust-motif in drama, poetry, the novel, films, and music runs to several volumes and is incomplete.

We touch here on deep, perhaps troubling waters. Why this economy of invention? I have put forward the hazardous conjecture that the primal Greek myths coincide, in some ways, with the origins of Indo-European grammar. Tales of uncertain or disputed identity would echo the gradual, halting determination of the first and second person singular; the legend of Helen's innocent stay in Egypt while only her exact shadow inhabited and doomed Troy, might preserve traces of the development of those truly fantastic grammatical resources known as 'if' clauses and counter-factuals. Whatever the reason, the fact is that only one fundamental story-theme has been added to the classical stock (Goethe himself adverted to the derivation of Faust from Prometheus). It is that of Don Juan, a theme inconceivable before Christian readings of sexuality and damnation. It is, moreover, distinctly possible that the mechanics of theme and variation, essential to music, are incised also in language and representation. It may be that a 'formulaic' way of telling the same story differently—observe our 'Westerns'—is an impulse of quasi-genetic force. When current 'Post-Modernism' declares that the 'time of the telling of the great stories is now over', it is worth remembering that the invention of these stories has been over for a considerable time. And that, as in the physics of 'strangeness', time in literature is reversible: the *Odyssey* now comes after *Ulysses* (cf. Borges) and the argonauts of Greek and Hellenistic epics follow on 'Star-Trek'.

Let me repeat: a persistent engagement with natural languages, an inquiry into the reception and influence of texts, an awareness of thematic analogies and variants, are part of all literary studies. In comparative literature, these concerns and their creative interactions are given particular emphasis. It is in the light of this emphasis that I would want, again on an obviously personal basis, to point to some areas of further exploration and development in the field.

European knowledge, European habits of argument and recognition, arise out of the transmission of classical antiquity and Hellenism to the West. This transmission turns on the role of Islamic philosophy and science in Mediterranean Europe. It tells, notably in certain regions of Spain and the Languedoc of a unique moment of coexistence between Islam, Judaism, and Christianity, between Hebrew, Arabic, and Latin and its vulgate descendants. (Europe was not to know this armistice of spirit again.) We lack, almost scandalously, scholars, intellectual and literary historians or critics, capable of reading or judging the Islamic material in its penetration of European Latinity. It is my amateurish belief that this lack has caused severe gaps and distortions in our maps of feeling and of thought. It is my guess that far more than medicine, natural sciences, and philosophic fragments from the ancient Greek made the crossing. Despite Islamic iconoclasm (so often exaggerated in Western accounts), shards, maybe more, of Greek literature, buried perhaps within quotations, reached the medieval ear. (I see no other way of accounting for Chaucer's association of Antigone with 'her sad song' or *threnos*.) Here, so much work lies before us.

This is true, as well, of the whole domain of Neo-Latin. In successive lexical and grammatical guises, Latin continues to be central to European law, politics, philosophy, science, and literature from the time of the collapse of the Roman Empire to the later nineteenth century. It is, quite obviously, the idiom of philosophical and scientific proposal, debate, and critique from Aquinas to Leibniz, from Roger Bacon to Copernicus, Kepler and Newton. Academic theses are composed and 'defended' in Latin. But so is literature. This ubiquity comprises dramas, lyrics, satires, epic poems composed in Latin from Portugal to Poland. Latin is the motor for Milton's reach outside England. Baudelaire can, does write Latin verse, as do Tennyson or Hopkins. But the effect, the aura is much larger. It is scarcely possible to interpret coherently the rhetoric of European literatures, the key notions of sublimity, of satire, of laughter which they embody and articulate without a just awareness of the Latin 'implication', of the unbroken, often almost subconscious negotiations of intimacy or of distance between the author in the vulgate and the Latin mould. This is as decisive for Dante as it is for Swift or Dryden; it is as crucial to Corneille as it is to Valéry. As it happens, Neo-Latin can be exceedingly difficult. The brute fact that relatively few among us can deal with it adequately has left a hollow near the very pivot of European comparative studies. Here, as well, necessary and fascinating work lies ahead.

A poem, a play, a novel can never be separated altogether from the illustrations or other pieces of art which it inspires, from its settings to music, from the films, radio-versions, television treatments which are based on it. Roman Jakobson called this motion of a text across other media 'transmutations'. These seem to me vital to the disciplines of understanding and valuation in comparative literature. Elsewhere, I have sought to show that different musical settings of the same Goethe or Eichendorff lyric by Schubert, Schumann, and Hugo Wolf constitute a compelling process of hermeneutic and critical 'placement' (F. R. Leavis's word, so precisely echoed in 'setting'). Verdi's *Otello* and *Falstaff* have a close, as it were exponential relation to the understanding of Shakespeare in late-romantic Europe. The lives of *Hamlet* are also those of the very different operas, films, paintings, even ballets which the play has generated. For generations of continental readers, Coleridge's 'Ancient Mariner' was the haunting product of Doré's illustrations. Today, exact technical reproducibility, electronic encoding and transmission, and, before long, the graphic-aural technologies of 'virtual reality' will bear, in ways nearly unpredictable, on the reception of language and of language in literature. Comparative studies are certain to proceed from an informing sense of metamorphosis to one of mutation. But was this not already the case when Greek vase-painters imaged Orpheus or Achilles, when Daumier painted Don Quixote, or when Liszt composed his purely instrumental 'translations' of Petrarch?

In the weeks to come, I will be lecturing on 'The Song of the Sirens', from archaic Greece to Joyce, Kafka, and Magritte. In part, I have chosen this thematic introduction precisely because of the seminal role of music and the arts. Iconography, as practised by Aby Warburg, Panofsky, and the Courtauld tradition, the history and philosophy of music, in the modes of Adorno, are an elemental part of comparative literature.

Lastly, I would point to a rubric which is, I admit, a personal passion. Outside formal and mathematical logic, all philosophy, all metaphysics, is a deed of language. No philosophic argument or picture of the world can be divorced from the language, style, rhetoric, means of presentment and illustration in which it is stated. This is self-evident not only when we are seeking to understand and interpret such virtuosos of language and poetic recourse as Plato, Saint Augustine, Pascal, or Nietzsche. It is true of every philosophic–metaphysical–theological text. The political doctrines of a Hobbes or a Rousseau are integral to their 'stylistics', to the *techne*, to the pacing and dramatizations of their discourse. What pressures did his native Spanish, his acquired Dutch and Hebrew exercise on Spinoza's choice and construction of a marmoreally timeless Latin, of a Latin that infers the Greek of Euclid? Can we dissociate the singular voice of Wittgenstein's *Tractatus* from the history of the German aphorism, notably in Lichtenberg? Once more, matters of translation are pivotal. Exactly as in poetry, so in philosophy and metaphysics, terms and turns of phrase are compacted with a density of potential significations, of questions to themselves and to the reader which make of even the most 'literal', unguarded attempts at translation an intricate process of commentary. There is more than hyperbole in Heidegger's contention that inadequate or erroneous translations of the word 'being' or the verb 'to be' in ancient Greek have determined the intellectual and, it may be, political history of the West.

Here is an area in which every resource of the comparatist in reference to languages, to dissemination, to reception, and thematic *ricorso* comes into play. Even the most abstract thought, once it is verbalized (and can there be pre-verbal thought?), exhibits its idiom. It takes on 'a local habitation and a name'. To my mind, there is nothing at once more fascinating and conducive to hermeneutics than an endeavour to observe, to elucidate the 'intertextuality' of philosophy and poetics, to hear the music which inhabits thought.

*

The present moment in Europe is hardly consoling. The ideals, the pragmatic dreams abroad in 1945 have faded into rancorous bureaucracy. Almost incomprehensibly, after the massacres, after the devastation of 1914 to 1945, crazed nationalism, tribal hatreds, religious and ethnic intolerance blaze again: in the Balkans, in Northern Ireland, in the Basque country, and our inner cities. The notion of a European concord, except on a commercial, fiscal, or mercantile basis—and even here there is little accord—seems to recede from realistic expectations. There are ways in which the Channel is today wider than before, in which Britain, during the Renaissance, the Augustan age, or the romantic decades, was closer to continental Europe than it is today. In paradoxical ways, the status of English as the planetary tongue, as the only working 'esperanto' of science, trade, and finance, has further isolated England from the post-Latin and German heritage of mainland Europe.

It would be fatuous bombast to suppose that any individual plea or contribution, especially from within the suspect, because still partly sheltered, confines of the academic could make much difference. The vaunt of money and the mass-media mocks the voice of the intellectual—a designation which can itself be used only with a considerable measure of irony and of remorse. Who are we to preach to others? What vanity, what treason sadder than that of many a cleric in the face of political seduction or menace?

Nevertheless, the generosity which has established this chair, the collaboration intended between this programme in comparative literature and other branches of European studies, signal a positive resolve. The history of the organic relations between Britain and the Continent, of the relations—now wholly decisive of our future—between Western and Eastern Europe, the study of the foundations of spirit on which a potential European community could be built, are to have their place at Oxford. Duns Scotus and Erasmus are invited back.

There is in this project a modest but authentic hope. And if there is a chronic infirmity by which every teacher ought to be afflicted, it is, indeed, hope.